About the Author

Justin Brooke is the "Traffic Guy Millionaires Recommend" because he has been the "traffic guy" for Dan Kennedy, Russell Brunson, Stansberry Research, Agora Financial, and many others. You may have seen Justin speak on stage or you might have heard him interviewed on EOFire, Mixergy, and the 27 other podcasts that he has been on.

Justin got started with just $60 in Adwords in 2007. Within a year he turned that $60 into six figures. He later built IMScalable.com, a digital ad agency, with his wife Chaunna. They built IMScalable into a seven figure digital ad agency, and have made millions for their clients.

Over the years Justin has managed $10,000,000+ in ad spend, driven over 50,000 customer acquisitions, and is now passionate about training the 9,000+ students he has in his online ad buying school, AdSkills.com.

1

Introduction

What you're about to learn is, arguably, one of the hottest advertising strategies of the decade.

Retargeting has become so popular because it multiplies the effectiveness of every minute and every dollar you spend on marketing.

Business size doesn't matter either. Retargeting works for startups and Fortune 500 companies alike.

This is because you can start your first campaign for less than $100 or complement a multi-million dollar branding campaign.

Before we dive in, let me tell you how I came to be an expert on retargeting.

I don't know who was first, but around 2008-ish we all called it something different. Some guys called it remarketing, others fetchback targeting, and still others called it recycled traffic.

Google still insists on calling it remarketing. Way to go Google. One day it may pay off.

It wasn't until somewhere between 2010 - 2011 that the term retargeting became the main adopted phrase. Even though AdRoll, a leader in retargeting software, was founded in 2007, it didn't really become a leader until around 2010.

By 2012, I was writing blog posts and speaking on stages about the power of retargeting. People were very curious about how to use this new super profitable magic called Retargeting.

At that time I was using it to retarget my blog readers with my products, and it was working like gangbusters.

Then in 2015, Ryan Deiss founder of DigitalMarketer.com, announced at his super conference that retargeting was their standard practice. From then on it has been one of the hottest topics in online advertising. Almost all major ad networks offer some form of retargeting pixel now.

And virtually every major product seller is deploying some form of retargeting.

Shortly before Ryan's announcement, he hired me to train his top media buyer, Molly Pittman. Molly and I discussed much of what I am going to tell you here. She went on to become the star of the company and the rest is history.

Now, I'm not saying I deserve credit for her success. I was just a teensy pawn in her rise to the top. She was already a top person in their company and took her skills far beyond our calls together. She is a rock star. You can (and should) listen to her podcast called Perpetual Traffic, it's great stuff. https://www.digitalmarketer.com/category/podcast/

I've been a part of retargeting since before it was even a "thing" and have spent millions on retargeting ads. As well as having been interviewed by 20+ podcasts, presented on dozens of stages, and a prolific client list, including: Dan Kennedy, Russell Brunson, Stansberry Research, and many more.

I've been there, done that, and now spend all of my time traveling with my family and teaching others how to increase their online ad profits.

Before we jump into profits though…

I do think we need to cover some vernacular just so we are on the same page about a few things.

Pixel

A tiny bit of javascript or HTML image code, which fires a message back to the ad network or tracking tool a few bits of information. It also tags the user with a cookie.

Cookie

Not the eating kind, but a little piece of code that gets saved in a users browser software to identify them later. Not identify the user personally, but as the same user who did "x" actions last visit. Where "x" is equal to whatever info you are tracking in your ad network.

Pixel Pool

This is a group of users you have tagged with pixels and cookies. Sometimes also referred to as your retargeting audience. I also lump in email lists that are uploaded to Facebook, Google, or other ad networks as pixel pools.

Burn Pixel

This is a pixel you are placing to create a pixel pool of users you do NOT want to retarget with ads. For example, customers or unsubs.

Lookalikes

Look-a-like, meaning a user that is similar to the users in your pixel pool or email list. Ad networks may call these lookalikes or similar audiences or close match audiences. All the same thing. They are all expansions of your pixel pool.

With that out of the way, let's get to the part where you start turning these words into dollars in your bank account.

I think the best starting point is helping you avoid the common rookie mistakes. I made all of these mistakes myself and I've seen many of my consulting clients make the same mistakes.

2

The Basics

Let me start out by saying, this chapter was written to give complete beginners an overview of what retargeting is, how it works, and some basic guidelines they should know before getting started. If you already have experience buying ads online or have been buying ads online for more than 12 months, you can likely skip to the next chapter. With that said, let's dive in.

Google calls it "remarketing."

The rest of us call it "retargeting."

It works by inserting a few lines of code onto your website which then "tags" (cookies) your visitors as they land on your pages. This starts building your "audience" or some call it, your "cookie pool."

Wikipedia defines a "cookie" as…

A cookie, also known as an HTTP cookie, web cookie, or browser cookie, is a small piece of data sent from a website and stored in a user's web browser while a user is browsing a website.

When the user browses the same website in the future, the data stored in the cookie is sent back to the website by the browser to notify the website of the user's previous activity.

Cookies were designed to be a reliable mechanism for websites to remember the state of the website or activity the user had taken in the past. This can include clicking particular buttons, logging in, or a record of which pages were visited by the user even months or years ago.

The code you place on your website is given to you by the network you choose to use. Today there are a lot of networks. I'll review them later in this book.

After you place the code on your website, you upload ads (banner ads and text ads) to the network. I'll also show you what these look like, best practices, and sizes later in this book.

The networks use the code you placed on your website to cookie your visitors. Once you have amassed an audience (cookie pool) they display your banner ads all over the internet, but only to people in your cookie pool. Your website visitors will feel like your ads are everywhere. When, in fact, they only appear everywhere because they have visited your website.

How does it work? Simple. The ad networks that provide the code to you and display your banners have relationships with hundreds of thousands of sites that allow the ad networks to show your ads all over the web. Some of these sites include USAToday, YouTube, Forbes, MTV, and thousands of smaller sites you've never heard about. If you're paying attention you just realized that YOU could have YOUR ADS on sites like USA Today, Forbes, and MTV.

What's So Great About Retargeting?

Imagine a visitor visits one of your web pages. They searched a keyword in Google and happen to find your page. Just as they are about to click onto your order page, their kid spills a bowl of Spaghett-o's, and off they go to solve this crisis.

Later that night they're reading the USA Today or watching Youtube videos and all of a sudden they see an ad for your product.

BOOM! They just remembered you and clicked back to your order page. This is the magic of retargeting. This is how it multiplies the effectiveness of EVERY minute and EVERY dollar you spend on marketing.

The beauty of retargeting is that you can use it to maximize ANY type of marketing campaign. You can retarget your email subscribers, Facebook ads, JV promotions, SEO, blog articles, and any other marketing channel.

The reason seasoned advertisers love it so much is because it solves the famous Thomas Smith problem. According to Thomas Smith who wrote a guide called Successful Advertising in 1885:

- The first time an ad appears, most don't even see it.
- The second time, they don't notice it.
- The third time, they are aware that it is there.
- The fourth time, they have a fleeting sense that they've seen it somewhere before.
- The fifth time, they actually read the ad.

Anyway, it continues all the way until the twentieth time when they finally buy your product. He may not have it down to a science, but the point is that the more times someone sees your ad, the more likely that person is to buy from you. And that's the beauty of retargeting.

You are showing ads to people who - you know for a fact - have already shown interest in what you are selling. It keeps your brand on the top of their mind. It allows you to follow up with them without needing them to opt-in or fill out a lead form. Do me a favor and read that last line again.

Six months down the road when you release a new product or have a special deal, you have a built in audience to market it too. Your ads are all over the web for your new product - overnight, or at least it seems that way to the viewers. The rest of the world doesn't know anything has happened, which is why some are calling it the "Invisible List."

Are There Any Downsides?

Before I continue, I want to address the controversial aspects of retargeting. Some people see it as an invasion of privacy. They don't like the idea of being "tagged" and followed. It creeps them out. However, we don't have any identifiable information on them. It's just an anonymous cookie being dropped into their browser that allows their browser to remember which pages they have visited. For this, people have been bashing "cookies," which are the codes we use to 'tag' users for retargeting.

Cookies Are Not Evil, Evil People
Who Use Cookies For Evil Are Evil

I love cookies… The kind you can eat and the kind your browser uses for retargeting. Never met a cookie I didn't like.

- Cookies are how my browser remembers my username and passwords—which I have hundreds of.
- Cookies are how my browser knows how to auto-complete my address into order forms.
- Cookies are how Facebook and Gmail remember me, so I don't have to friggin login every time.
- Cookies are how my affiliate links are tracked, so I get paid.
- Cookies are also how certain websites choose which ads to show me, which is where retargeting comes in.

Thanks to cookies, I see ads that pertain to me. I see ads for things that may have interested me (that I've completely forgotten about) instead of ads that are not relevant to me. Some people don't like them and because of that, there are settings for each browser, whether it's Firefox, Explorer, Safari or Chrome, that can prevent companies from slapping cookies on users and 'tagging' them with their codes.

As a marketer or business owner, you should love cookies. I once had a large potential client tell me that he uses "Ad Blockers" on his computer. I stopped the conversation and told him he should hire someone else. You can't be a deer hunter and a vegetarian.

Long story short, there will be some people out there that hate cookies and have their security settings turned up higher than Fort Knox.

Retargeting Will Get Harder

The next thing you need to know is that retargeting will get harder (and may even go away) soon. There is a war going on right now between privacy advocates and Internet browsers like Chrome, Firefox, and Internet Explorer.

They have started a "Do Not Track" movement. At the time of writing this, all PC computers shipped with Windows 8 are default set to block cookies! Mozilla, maker of the Firefox browser is doing all they can to help remind all of their users how to turn off cookie tracking as well as opt-out of whole networks from tracking their actions. Not to mention all the plugins and softwares that are being developed to fight, block, fool, and deny cookie tracking. It is very much like pop-up advertising back in the day and all of the pop-up blockers. Except, I don't believe retargeting ads to be anywhere near as invasive as pop-up ads were.

Beyond browsers and plugins, you have the General Data Protection Regulations (GDPR) coming out of the EU, which will likely spread to other countries and become common practice. This is new privacy regulation that goes into a LOT of detail. I'm not a lawyer, so I'll let you consult legal counsel on how to implement this for your business. My job is to simply let you know about it.

While retargeting is getting hard, it still works and it's working incredibly well. However, we're all wondering how this browser cookie/tracking war is going to play out. Will retargeting survive? I hope so, because I'm seeing 300%+ ROI on some campaigns. You should get started as soon as you can before the window closes.

Now that you know what to watch out for, let's discuss the some mistakes many make when starting their retargeting campaigns.

3

Rookie Mistakes

After creating hundreds, probably thousands of retargeting campaigns and helping AdSkills students over the years, I've created a list of common mistakes businesses make when they start retargeting. Here are the three most common:

Rookie Retargeting Mistake #1

Don't retarget too many people. The point of retargeting is to have a really high quality pixel pool to show ads too. If you are retargeting everyone the same, then you lose the effectiveness of retargeting.

Just like with your email list, you don't want crappy leads that buy nothing, right?

Well, even more so with retargeting because you are paying to retarget those crappy users. Instead, start with the smallest - most likely to buy - audience. For example, dropping a pixel on your Shopping Cart page and a burn pixel on your Thank You page.

Now you can retarget just the people who almost bought but didn't quite pull the trigger. This is one of my easy money recipes that I start every client with.

Rookie Retargeting Mistake #2

Don't make your ads creepy. Consumers get a little creeped out if your ads say "Hey remember me from yesterday?" or "Hey I saw you visited this page last week."

The only person who thinks that is clever is you. The customer thinks "OMG! What else were they tracking? Who else is tracking me? I feel like a piece of meat in a lion's cage."

Instead, be subtle. They already know they were on your page yesterday. You don't need to say that. Save all that space to tell them the benefits of your product. You know, the one they looked at yesterday.

Rookie Retargeting Mistake #3

Don't overdo it. Subtlety is the key. If I leave your website and then everywhere I go I see five ads for your product, it gets offensive and smells of desperation.

Also, same goes for retargeting for too long. Just because the ad network saves the pixel for 540 days does not mean that's how long you should show your ads to the pixel pool. In all my testing and millions spent, I find that after 30 days there is a diminishing return on investment.

Instead, set your frequency cap to 3 per day and campaign flight date to 30 days. You can adjust these settings a little to fit your needs, but let it be a starting point.

Besides, if they are seeing your ad 3x a day for 30 days and still don't buy, then it's time for a new ad anyway. I should point out here that I'm not saying you should stop showing ads past 30 days, just not the same ad for 30+ days.

If you stopped reading here and all you did was avoid those three mistakes, you would do better than most businesses.

But I don't want you to be just a smidge above average. I pride myself on my readers being the alpha lions of online ads. In these next few chapters I'm going to start showing you how to dominate your market with retargeting.

I will show you the best tools to use the best ad networks, how to exploit these tools and networks, plus advanced campaign schemes that squeeze out every drip of ROI.

Beginner's note:
Two more words you can add to your retargeting dictionary are:

- **Frequency cap** - a limit you can place on how many times ad networks will show your ads within a 24 hour period.

- **Campaign flight date** - the time frame you set to run a campaign for within an ad network.

4

Retargeting Deployment Tools & Ad Networks

I know you are itching to get to the fun part where we design sexy retargeting ads. And I tell you my super secret campaign setting for unlocking ROI from your campaigns. Trust me, it's all coming.

I have taught this for a long time. There is a sequence it must be taught in for you to get the best results. Right now, we need to talk about retargeting deployment tools and ad networks.

Best Deployment Tools & Networks

First you need a tag management tool. There's going to be lots of codes you need to place on your pages. Instead of writing for your web guy or manually placing codes (which often leads to errors) you'll want a way to rapidly deploy these codes.

Google Tag Manager (GTM for short) is the tool I use and recommend. It's free and one of the most powerful tools a modern marketer can use today. Plus, there's a ton of 3rd party support for it; consultants, Fiverr gigs, courses, YouTube videos, etc.

With GTM, you can place one bit of code on all pages and then with a click of your mouse deploy or hide all the various pixels we will be using. Plus, you can also do advanced trigger rules so that your codes are delayed or even fired by a specific page event.

I'm not even going to try to explain step-by-step how to sign up for and setup GTM. I won't waste your time or insult your intelligence with that drivel.

I, personally, like the MeasureSchool Youtube channel for all things related to tracking, analytics, and data. That's where I learned how to setup GTM and do all kinds of advanced hacks with it. My business partner and fellow AdSkills instructor John is a master at tracking and analytics. He's working on additional training for media buyers on our AdSkills YouTube channel as well.

If you want someone else to handle your GTM set up, you can hire AdSkills students I've trained that now provide this as a done for you service in our marketplace. Just go to AdSkills.com/providers.

The next tool I use for tracking is Google Analytics. Google Analytics is a free tracking software. If you already have Google Analytics on all your pages, great. If not, now you can easy do so with Google Tag Manager. You'll want to install Google Analytics on all your pages since it is the only way to use Google Ads remarketing features.

You use Google Analytics to create audiences and then in Google Ads you set up ads to advertise to those audiences. We'll talk more about audience development later.

Lastly, I recommend making sure you have active ad accounts with Facebook, Twitter, Adwords, and Taboola. You'll understand more about why later. The gist of it is you want your retargeting to show up everywhere like a blanket over the Internet. These 4 ad networks let you cover roughly 98% of the Internet with ads.

The problem with most rookies is they only do retargeting in Facebook or AdRoll or just Google Ads. This is far less effective because it leaves huge gaps in where your user can "disappear" and find other advertisers to fall in love with.

If you are only retargeting on Facebook, and I am in your niche using all four networks I'm going to win because I'll have a more efficient coverage.

I have found there is a weird effect that happens when you are everywhere versus in one channel. Meaning, if you are showing up in multiple places you can actually spend less and get similar or better results than if you were in just one spot.

For example, imagine if they saw your ad on TV, then a billboard on the way to the grocery store, then again in the newspaper they bought. Finally, you showed up as a radio ad on the way home. Now, all of that traditional advertising would cost a fortune to have such a blanketing strategy, but online you can create the same effect for just $100/day.

Let's recap:

1. Google Tag Manager lets you have one central location for all your pixels. You can add users, assign permissions, rapidly deploy pixels, and do advanced triggers. All of this for free. Thanks, Google.

2. Google Analytics lets you create audiences based on many factors including: page, session length, geolocation, referrer, and many more. As well as audiences based on a mix of those different factors. Again, all for free.

3. Facebook, Twitter, Taboola, and Google Ads are the four corners of the Internet letting you create a true blanket retargeting campaign. With these four networks you will show up virtually everywhere your audience visits online including; social networks, articles, web pages, forums, emails, even YouTube. And you can do it all for less than $100/day.

In fact, let's move on to budgeting.

5

Budgeting for Small & Large Spends

There are two budgeting strategies you can use; one for small budgets and another for big budgets.

First, you need to understand how money gets allocated to retargeting campaigns. It is different from normal ad campaigns.

In a normal ad campaign you set a max bid and daily or lifetime budget. Then, an auction happens between you and every other advertiser vying for the same audience. The winner is whoever has the best combination of Click Through Rate (CTR), Relevance, and Cost Per Click (CPC) bid.

With retargeting, it's different since you are only advertising to those who you have already pixeled on your site.

That means if you only have 1000 people pixeled, you literally can't spend a lot of money. Your budget is limited to how large your pixel pool is, which is another great reason to filter who you pixel down to the best qualified visitors.

It's not until you get up to 10,000 pixeled users or higher that you can even begin to "scale" your retargeting budget.

That is actually the one big downside of retargeting. While it is very profitable, you are limited by the size of your pixel pool. Meaning if you are making $3 for every $1 you spend (a home run), you can't just throw more money at it to grow it. You must first grow your pixel pool.

With that said, here are the two budgeting strategies I suggest for maximum spread and profit.

Smaller Budgets

For smaller budgets, it is hard to slice up the pie. There is only so much budget that can go around. For example, if your budget is $100/day I suggest an even split across all four ad networks. There is a 5th, that we will talk about that soon, but for now let's just assume Facebook, Twitter, Google Ads, and Taboola. That's $25/day on each.

If you were to try to manipulate the percentages at these low budget levels, you would just handicap yourself. Instead, for low budgets you need the maximum % per network.

Larger Budgets

When it comes to larger budgets, say in the $1,000+/day level, you should manipulate the percentages based on the size of network. For example, I would put 40% to 60% towards Google Ads and then split the rest on the other 3. Or maybe Facebook is very good for your market and you spend 40% on Facebook and 40% on Google Ads and then just 10% each on Twitter and Taboola.

When you have enough budget that you can split up the percentages and still have substantial dollars, that is the ideal strategy for maximizing ROI.

This is because if you notice one network is getting you $3 per $1 and another is getting you $5 per $1 spent, you obviously want to allocate a higher percentage of the budget to the higher earning network. But you don't want to kill the other network either because it is still profitable.

Another reason for manipulating the percentages would be size of inventory. Google Ads is a very, very large ad network. Even if you have a small pixel pool, you have many different ways of showing retargeting ads in Adwords.

You have text ads, image ads, responsive ads, YouTube ads, and Gmail ads. That's why my default percentage spread is 40% to Google and 20% to the other three networks.

Lastly, this section wouldn't be complete without talking about bidding.

Bidding

The same rules apply for bidding on clicks with retargeting and normal campaigns. The only difference is that usually you can afford to bid a little higher with retargeting since it's a higher qualified click and higher converting campaigns.

With normal ad campaigns you are bidding on someone's first click. You don't even know if they will stay on your page longer than 30 seconds yet, so you should bid less for this type of click.

With retargeting, depending on your rules, you already know this is a qualified visitor. This person is on their 2nd or 3rd click so they are worth a higher bid.

Okay, that's the last of the setup and knowledge section. You should now have a decent foundation when it comes to retargeting. Next, we get into example ads, best practices, and specific retargeting recipes you can copy in your campaigns for higher ROI.

6

Retargeting Ad Design & Layout

The first example ad I'll cover is called, "The Workhorse" (see next page). I have personally spent over one million dollars on this exact model for both retargeting and cold traffic. It works (hence the name), and if you do your research you will also see a lot of top media buyers using it.

This ad has seven important parts to it:
1. Image
2. White Background
3. Headline
4. Description
5. Branding
6. Call to Action
7. Border

As you can see, there really is no special design to it. These can literally be made in Powerpoint or Paint. You don't even need to get a designer involved.

It's important that you know the branding and border are there for very specific reason. If you do not include these your ads may be limited on which sites they can and cannot appear on. This is because of the IAB (International Advertising Bureau) has guidelines that ads must follow. It is not a law as they are not a legal authority, however, most of the top sites adhere to their guidelines.

The border and branding is there to let the consumer know that this is a separate "thing" from the rest of the site, and not part of the actual site. If you do not include these, the FTC could have a case for saying you are using deceptive marketing. So please, just leave the thin border and branding. The marginal boost in CTR you get from not having it is not worth the hassle.

I don't advise changing the colors and fonts too much. Arial, Helvetica, Droid Sans, Myriad Pro, or Verdana are the recommended fonts. For the headline, you can test red, black, or blue. I wouldn't stray much from that. I have tested many colors, and those three are the majority winners. Now obviously this specific ad is not a "retargeting" ad. It is an interest-building ad designed for cold traffic as a first touch. What I wanted to show you about the ad was the layout and design style.

To make this an effective retargeting ad you would;
1. Update the image section with a picture of your product.
2. Make thehe headline your main benefit.
3. Then, make the descriptiona summary of what problem your product is a solution for.
4. And finally, the call to action link would be "Buy Now" or "Finish Checkout" or "Add To Cart."

I shouldn't have to tell you, but I don't want this to be overlooked -- **split test these elements.**

The image section should be a picture of your product
Headline Should Be Your Main Benefit
The description should be a summary of the problem your product is a solution too. And the call to action link would be "Buy Now" or "Finish Checkout" or "Add To Cart."
YourDomain.com   Add To Cart

* You should split test the image, headline, description and CTA in this retargeting ad

That, in a nutshell, is a basic retargeting ad. It's important to understand that when I say "basic," I don't mean sub-par. I mean that is the bar you must meet to have a good retargeting ad. You rarely need to do more than this, but in the next section I'll describe a few advanced retargeting ad variations you can try (for even more profits).

7

Advanced Retargeting
Ad Strategies

There are four types of retargeting ad strategies in my arsenal. Other guys may have others and that's cool. We all have our own way of doing things. These are the four that work best for me and the 9,000 students in AdSkills.

1. The Brander
2. The Product Reminder
3. The Instant Celebrity
4. The Fence Jumper

#1 The Brander

This ad is usually only used after you have attempted all the other strategies. The goal of this ad is to just keep your brand in the target customer's awareness. Maybe they'll come back.

- The Image should be your logo and slogan. Maybe a picture of your storefront if you have one or whatever other imagery of your business you think is significant.

- The Headline is the core benefit of what your company helps people with.

- The Description is a credibility statement like "As seen in..." or "5,000 business owners trust us for..." etc.

- Call to action is "learn more" or "read more."

The purpose of this ad is just to keep the audience from growing cold on you. They'll be ready to buy one day, and when they do you'll be glad this ad was still running. It's the catch-all ad for people who were just mildly interested at first visit but have yet to convert.

#2 The Product Reminder

This is the workhorse ad of retargeting. This is the one you've seen most other companies using. The goal of this ad is to remind the viewer of the product they were recently viewing.

- The Image is a picture of the product.

- The Headline is the main benefit of the product (should be split-tested).

- The Description is a summary of the problem your product solves.

- The Call to action is "Buy Now" or "Order Now" or "Add to Cart" etc.

Not everyone has their wallet on them the moment they find out about your product. Or maybe they had to ask their spouse, or maybe they wanted to wait until payday. The purpose of this ad is to remind them about the product they were interested in. This ad should be the first touch ad of your retargeting program.

#3 The Instant Celebrity

I can't say I invented this, but I am the first person I've ever seen use this type of retargeting ad. Now I see tons of companies using it. And they should. When it works it's a windfall of profit. The goal is to make it look like the whole Internet is saying good things about you.

- The Image consists of pictures of your customers or whoever is endorsing you.

- The Headline is a summary of their testimonial/endorsement.

- The Description is a sentence raving about one aspect of your product.

- The Call to action is "Learn More" or "Read More" or "Get One Now."

The purpose of this ad is to have reviews, testimonials, and endorsements for your product everywhere the prospect visits. If they go on Facebook, they see testimonials. If they go to Twitter, they see testimonials. If they go to YouTube, or anywhere on the web... testimonials! This ad can also be a first touch, or it can be a third touch, maybe just before resorting to the Brander ad.

#4 The Fence Jumper

I wanted to call this one "The Cardone" because up until his ad worked on me, I just had the other three retargeting ad types. His worked so well on me that I immediately started adding it to my clients' campaigns. It worked like a charm. The Fence Jumper made pixel pools I thought were dead all of a sudden spring alive.

The goal is to offer an irresistible deal on the product they were thinking of buying, but have not for whatever reason.

- The Image should be a picture of the product, but with a high contrast overlay saying "Sale" or "Discount" or "Now only $xx."

- The Headline should say "For Limited Time Now Only $xx."

- The Description should explain why it's now on sale. Come up with a reason such as Spring Sale, Easter Sale, Winter Sale, Summer Sale, Back to School Sale, whatever.

- The Call to action says "Buy Now" or "Add to Cart" or "Claim Offer."

The purpose of this ad is to go out 15 to 30 days after the Product Reminder or instant celebrity ad has run. We'll talk about message sequencing later, but this ad type is a cleanup ad. It's meant to come in after another ad and round up all the stragglers for a new burst of sales.

Try not to think of it as a discount, and think about it more as revenue that was about to be lost, but is now captured.

Okay, now that you know the different ad types, let's get into the campaigns you can use these different ads with. The recipes below are exactly that, recipes for where to place your pixels, what type of ads to run, and for how long.

8

Retargeting Recipes For ROI

What we discuss next are the recipes the whole title of this book comes from. These are blueprints for retargeting campaigns you can implement in your business and get great results from. I've also put them in order of which you should do first and then scale up by adding each of the others.

If you just skip to the end and try to add the biggest baddest one, good luck. Maybe you're a great white shark and can swim in the deepest waters. If not, follow the process and start with the first recipe first.

Recipe #1: The Cart Fixer

If you sell a product or service, you likely have a shopping cart software. Maybe it's Infusionsoft or Samcart or Thrivecart or Gumroad or whatever. This recipe is agnostic of the type of cart you have. As long as you have one, this recipe will fix your cart abandonment rate.

This is the one I start every client, business, or student out on because it's the surest to generate profits and incorporates the three key skills necessary for being good at retargeting.

The Recipe:

- Pixel people on your order page.
- Exclude or burn pixel people on your thank you page.
- Run the Product Reminder ad from day 1 to 30 days.
- Budget for this is $50 - $500/day depending on cart volume.

Recipe #2: The Blog Monetizer

If you have a blog, podcast, or advertorial, this campaign is great for turning your readers into customers. Mad props if you use this to increase your Patreon earnings.

The Recipe:

- Pixel people on your content pages.
- Exclude or burn pixel any customers.
- Run either The Instant Celebrity or Product Reminder ad from day 1 - 30.
- Run the Fence Jumper from day 31 - 45.
- Run the Brander from day 46 - ongoing.
- Budget for this is a steady $10 - $25/day.

Recipe #3: The Instant Celebrity

This recipe works for any product, but is especially good for service sellers and coaches. The key is having multiple testimonials across multiple ad networks. It's supposed to look like lots of people saying good things about you all over the web. Ideally, different people in different places i.e. Twitter, Facebook, YouTube, etc.

The Recipe:

- Pixel people on all your landing/blog/website pages.
- Exclude or burn pixel people on your confirmation page.
- Run multiple Instant Celebrity ads from day 1 - 14.
- Piggy back the Product Reminder ad to anyone who clicks.
- Budget for this is $25 - $100/day depending on traffic volume.
- DO NOT run this recipe and Blog Monetizer together. Choose one.

Recipe #4: The Face-To-Face

The benefit of digital marketing is how fast, cheap, and trackable it is. However, the biggest downside is how impersonal it can be. Most people just use text ads, sales pages and at best, group webinars.

What if you could look your visitor in the eye, and introduce yourself with all the same body language and vocal inflection of being in person - but virtually?

The purpose of this recipe is to follow up a visit to your website with a personal video introduction. This method allows you to better explain your offer, company, and why they should buy from you.

The Recipe:

- Pixel people on sales pages.
- Exclude or burn pixel people on your confirmation page.
- Run a video ad introducing yourself from day 1 through 3.
- Run a fence jumper ad from day 4 - 7.
- Budget for this is $25 - $250/day depending on traffic volume.
- DO NOT run this recipe with the Greased Funnel. Choose one.
- GREAT in combination with the Blog Monetizer.

Recipe #5: The Microwave

A.K.A., The Volleyball Campaign I wrote about in my Daily Edge newsletter (adskills.com/edge). Originally, this was explained to me by my good friend, Curt Maly at BlackBoxSocialMedia.com.

The purpose is to quickly and cheaply filter out the not-so-interested people from the interested using a video ad. You can then retarget people who watched most of the video. This turns cold traffic into warm traffic literally within minutes.

The Recipe:

- Target the broadest but still relevant audience possible.
- Run a video ad on Facebook or YouTube. 3-5 mins of pure content works best.
- Run a Product Reminder ad to anyone who watched 50%+ from day 1 - 14.
- Run a Fence Jumper ad from day 15 - 30.
- Exclude or burn pixel anyone who purchases your product.
- Budget $100 - $1,0000/day for the video and $25 - $100/day for the other ads.

Recipe #6: The Greased Funnel

This recipe helps mediocre funnels become better funnels, and turns good funnels into absolute monsters. The purpose of this recipe is to give your visitors a little nudging along each step of your funnel in case they idle too long at one step. This is the first audience laddering campaign introduced.

Audience Ladder:

1. Landing page pixel
2. Sales page pixel
3. Cart page pixel
4. Upsell page pixels

The Recipe:

- Create a pixel for each step of your funnel.
- Create a burn pixel or exclusion rule for each step of your funnel.
- Run a customized Product Reminder ad for each step of the funnel from days 1 - 7.
- Budget $5 - $25/day per funnel step.
- DO NOT run this recipe and Cart Fixer together. Choose one.
- DO NOT pixel downsell pages if you have them. It's overkill.

Recipe #7: The Webinar Assistant

People can ignore reminder emails, but they cannot ignore reminder ads all across the web. The purpose of this recipe is to increase webinar registrations, attendance, and sales. It is a very advanced recipe that requires combining message sequencing and audience laddering.

Audience Ladder:

1. Registration page pixel
2. Confirmation page pixel
3. Replay page pixel

The Recipe Part 1:

- Pixel people who visit your registration page.
- Exclude or burn pixel people on your confirmation page.
- Run the Product Reminder ad from days 1 - 3.
- Budget $25 - $100/day depending on traffic volume.

The Recipe Part 2:

- Pixel people who land on your confirmation page.
- Manually turn on a Product Reminder ad (for the webinar) 24 hours before the event.
- Manually pause the Product Reminder ad after the event.
- Manually turn on a Product Reminder ad (for the re-play) for 24 - 72 hours after the event.
- Budget $10 - $50/day depending on registration volume.

IMPORTANT NOTE: Budgets are low because there is typically only 100 - 1,000 webinar attendees. If you have mega webinars with 5,000+ attendees just 5x the recommended budget. $100/day goes a LOOONG way for pixel pools smaller than 10,000 people.

Recipe #8: The Earnings Multiplier

I came up with this recipe by asking myself, "If direct mail legends like Gary Halbert, Eugene Schwartz, and Claude Hopkins were still around today, how would they use retargeting?" I took strategies that old school guys used and modernized them with current technology.

The purpose of this recipe is to use an old database marketing concept, RFM (Recency, Frequency, & Monetary), to serve different ads to your different types of customers. Instead of pixels, you will use custom audiences. You will use these different levels and custom audiences to higher earnings.

Audience Ladder:

1. Leads-only custom audience
2. All-customers custom audience
3. 1 purchase only custom audience
4. Multi-purchase customers custom audience
5. Top 20% spenders custom audience

The Recipe Part 1

- Target your leads-only custom audience.
- Exclude anyone who is on all-customers custom audience.
- Run a Fence umper ad from days 1 - 30.
- Budget for this is $25 - $250/day depending on how many leads you have.
- DO NOT run this recipe with other recipes currently running.

The Recipe Part 2

- Target your 1 purchase only custom audience
- Exclude anyone who is on multi-purchase customers custom audience
- Run a Fence Jumper ad (for all products) from day 1 - 30
- Budget for this is $25 - $50/day depending on audience size

The Recipe Part 3

- Target your top 20% spenders custom audience
- Run a Product Reminder ad (for high ticket offer) from days 1 - 30
- Budget for this is $25 - $50/day depending on audience size.

With these seven recipes you'll be better equipped than 90% of other retargeting marketers who are doing just basic retargeting. Each of these recipes are designed for profit. Do not stretch the budgets or time frames unless you have MUCH larger audiences than average companies.

These budgets and timeframes were chosen strategically based on millions of dollars spent doing this for my clients and consulting with AdSkills students. Going over budget or over time will result in diminishing returns and lower ROI.

I have taken into account the way these network algorithms work at different spend levels and performance levels. If you adjust the budgets and time frames out of the scope in these recipes, you risk putting your campaigns into larger spending brackets or lower performing brackets which will greatly affect the end result.

You've been warned.

Lastly, you may be wondering about some of the phrases mentioned in these recipes. While I didn't invent "pixel laddering" or "message sequencing," I did give things in this book names that would be easy for us to remember and discuss.

In the next chapter, I'll cover my advanced retargeting concepts, the phrases I use for them, and a description of what they are. I also explain why you should be using them.

9

Advanced Retargeting Concepts

Unlike the recipes I mentioned previously, this section covers retargeting concepts. They can be used and interchanged inside of your recipes. All of them are important for you to know, and know how to use if you want to be great at retargeting.

In this section I'll explain the following:

1. Message sequencing
2. Audience ladders
3. Audience segmentation
4. Delayed pixel firing

Message Sequencing

Just like you have a series of messages you send new leads via email, you can and should be doing the same with your retargeting ads. Most people are just showing one ad, and showing it too often for too long. Retargeting as a "set it and forget it" strategy is a bad idea.

Instead you should have one ad that runs for "x" amount of days, another after it, and maybe another after that. A good basic message sequence for retargeting is first reminding them of the product. Then after a week or so offering a discount on the product they looked at. Finally, offering them a huge discount on the product they looked at.

Of course, you'll need to keep your margins in mind with these discounts. However, if used correctly message sequences can capture return on ad spend that would not have been realized without it. Another example of a message sequence would be showing different testimonials in The Instant Celebrity ad instead of just one. More testimonials creates more credibility and keeps the campaign fresh.

With Twitter and Facebook you can even create campaigns based on engagement with an ad. This way you could create a new message for someone who has already clicked versus someone who has not clicked yet.

Audience Ladder

Just like free leads are different from buyer leads, so are your different pixel pools. Instead of just having one retargeting audience, you should think in terms of creating an audience ladder.

Create one pixel pool, or custom audience of all visitors. Another for all customers. Another for all leads. You can then customize it to your own sales process. You could have an audience for single product purchasers, frequent buyers, unsubscribes, big spenders, etc.

This becomes a full time job for one person in the company to always be managing your different pixeled audiences, custom audiences, and audience ladder. Add to that, then making sure to always be running the right message sequencing to those audiences to move them up the ladder. As they move up the ladder your ROI begins to stack.

It's like compound investing. Where you got x% ROI on moving leads to the single product purchasers rung on the ladder, then you get y% ROI moving them to a multi-purchaser. All the way up to becoming a big spender. What's the initial ROI on that first campaign then? Frankly, I'm not good enough at math to tell you. What I do know is ,the more I focus on moving people up the ladder, the more revenue my company makes.

Audience Segmentation

Technically, an audience ladder is an audience segmentation, but I look at one as a vertical movement and the other as horizontal. For example, audience segmentation to me means having one pixel pool for all buyers of roduct A and another for product B. It could even be one pixel pool for everyone visiting category A of my blog versus category B of my blog.

On of the most important segmentation schemes I think every company should have is an RFM audience segmentation. Many have this for their email or direct mail lists. Why not for your pixel pools, too?

Imagine having an audience of customers who bought in the last 30 days versus customers whose last purchase was 90+ days out. The messaging to both would be very different right? So then doesn't it make sense to have both segmented out?

As covered earlier, RFM stands for recency, frequency, and monetary. It's an old database marketing concept for extracting the most money out of your database. Well, pixel pools are not much different than databases, in fact they are quite literally data points.

Delayed Pixel Fire

To give credit where credit is due, I first learned of this through my buddy Mike Rhodes, co-author of "The Ultimate Guide To Google Adwords."

Imagine you are pixeling everyone who comes to your sales page. Well, we know that people who leave in the first 30 seconds are "bounces." That means you are retargeting all those people who bounced, which could be as high as 60%. Meaning 60% of your retargeting budget is going to waste.

Instead, use Google Tag Manager to delay that retargeting pixel fire until after 30 seconds or even later to scrub that budget clean of all the bouncers. Now 100% of the retargeting budget is going to qualified engaged visitors.

Furthermore, if you have a video sales page or webinar replay page, you could delay the pixel all the way to the halfway point of your video. Now you can retargeting only people who were deeply engaged enough to watch at least half of your video. Delaying your pixel can be used in many ways and very profitably if you are clever.

10

Resources

In this section I've compiled a few resources you'll need when buying ads online including popular ad sizes, landing page best practices, as well as training and services available for getting your retargeting campaigns set up.

Popular Banner Ad Sizes

As I mentioned previously, I rely heavily on the 250x300 "medium square" because it has outperformed over other ad sizes time and again. Before writing this section, I researched the interwebs for additional data to back up my own personal experience. I was going to compile the data into the topic I originally outlined as, "Top 10 Most Effective Banner Ads." However, after reading through multiple reports, I found that 90% of ad impressions come down to just 3 sizes.

- The #1 being the medium rectangle (no surprise there),
- The #2 the leaderboard (728x90), followed by #3 the half page (300x600).

The Medium Rectangle

This is the most served banner size on the Google Display Network. It captures 1/3 of all served ad impressions with an average share of 33%. (This number varies depending on which report I found, but seemed to be consistently in the 30% range).

The Leaderboard

The leaderboard is popular because it fits perfectly in the site header of a website. While it has prominent placement on a website in the header, I'm still a big fan of the medium rectangle because those are often placed within the content that the visitor is reading. The leaderboard normally goes around the content. I'm not saying it isn't worth testing once you have an ad performing well in the medium rectangle size.

The Half Page

The half page is a wide vertical banner similar to the "skyscraper" banner which is only 160x600. They have basically just doubled the width giving you more space within the content to advertise. This ad unit is growing more and more popular and is often placed close to or within the content of the website. I believe this is why the half page ad size is growing in popularity.

Landing Page Best Practices

I know this is not a book about landing pages, but I would be remiss if I didn't share my tips on landing pages to help you increase conversions once you have your visitors coming back to your website. We have a full course on landing page layouts, but these are the seven elements I make sure to optimize when looking to improve landing conversions.

1. Relevance - Ensure that your copy is related to the interests of your market / target audience.

2. Identity - Does the page have common business identity details like a Logo, Business Name, Contact Details (Address, Phone, Email), and Privacy Policy?

3. Usability - Be sure that the page has an easy to identify next step. Is your action step (button) highlighted by a different color?

4. Credibility - Remember the website visitor likely has no clue who you are. Adding "As Seen On (related authority websites) and website trust logos help with showing your reputation.

5. Social Proof - Again, your visitor doesn't know you. Including testimonials will help to counter

this.

6. Urgency - Your visitor needs a reason to take action now. You can use verbiage to increase urgency. This can be a warning, limited availability, ending soon, etc.

7. Believability - Most importantly, all of the elements listed above need to be believable and realistic.

Optimization Process

I'm often asked, how do I know what to test? Amongst our team we created an optimization framework that we follow. Here is a quick breakdown of our process:

1. Ask yourself, "What is our mission?" Here you need to identify what you want to increase. Is it sales? Leads? Revenue? Once you've identified it, make a goal statement.

   Example: "Increase our Facebook sales by receiving orders for weight loss supplements subscription"

2. Next, ask yourself, "What will I test?" Identify elements that will help achieve your goal.

   Example: Increase CTR, reduce shopping cart abandonment, improve images

3. In this step you want to ask yourself, "How will I know we're winning?" Here you want to identify the metric of success (volume, ratio, percentages).

   Example: # of new subscriptions

4. Lastly, ask yourself," How will I know when I'm finished?" In this step, you'll need to find your end target for the optimization test. This doesn't have to be the "end" of your optimization, just the "test" to see if you do "x" will you get "y" result.

   Example: 37 orders sold in Month 1, new monthly target = 100

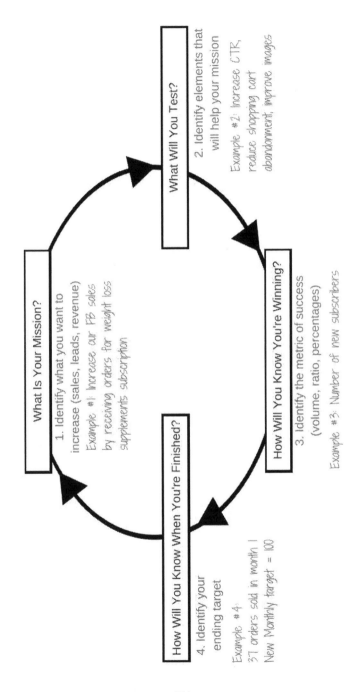

What Is Your Mission?

1. Identify what you want to increase (sales, leads, revenue)

Example #1: Increase our FB sales by receiving orders for weight loss supplements subscription

What Will You Test?

2. Identify elements that will help your mission

Example #2: Increase CTR, reduce shopping cart abandonment, improve images

How Will You Know You're Winning?

3. Identify the metric of success (volume, ratio, percentages)

Example #3: Number of new subscribers

How Will You Know When You're Finished?

4. Identify your ending target

Example #4:
37 orders sold in month 1
New Monthly target = 100

74

Final Words

Thank you for reading *Retargeting Recipes*. I'm sure you've found it helpful if you have never run a campaign yourself. If you have, then it's just a good reminder of the important things to know.

For some people, after reading they realize one of two things:

> a) They need someone with experience who can help guide them through setting up their first campaigns and helping to make them profitable. OR...

> b) They want someone with experience to run these campaigns for them.

The good news is I can help you with both of those decisions.

Since 2015, I've been working hard to improve the media buying education available for professional ad buyers through my speaking, podcast interviews, blog posts, and courses. In 2016 I launched AdSkills.com, an online school for media buyers. At AdSkills, our goal is to improve the training for media buyers. We also help pair media buyers with businesses based on their budget and experience requirements.

If you want to hire an experienced media buyer to set up the retargeting campaigns I've covered in this book, we have a team of experts media buyers who are waiting to set them up for you. All you have to do to get started is visit AdSkills.com/providers to select a Media Buyer I've trained.

OR, you can fill out our Media Buyer Matchmaking form and we'll find a media buyer to match your goals and budget for you at adskills.com/media-buyers-for-hire

Whether you decide to hire a media buyer I've trained or pass this book on to one of your team members to start implementing these strategies for your business, it doesn't matter to me. My only hope is that you start implementing and let us know how it goes. I wish you nothing but success in all your marketing campaigns.

As I end this book, I just want to say thank you again. Be sure to keep your eyes open for more new releases from AdSkills in the near future. We have a lot more knowledge to share with you. If you want to receive all our updates and free tips join the Edge at AdSkills.com/edge

Talk Soon,
Justin Brooke